So You've Been Asked To Pray

Dr. John B. Toay

and

Woody Young

Joy Publishing
San Juan Capistrano, California

So You've Been Asked To Pray © 1991 Joy Publishing

Special permission is granted for individual use of a prayer or a complete *Kit-Cat* drawing and caption as long as it is used in proper context and not-for-profit environment (ie. church bulletin). Drawings may not be separated from captions without written permission.

No part of this book may be reproduced or transmitted in any form or by any means, electronic or mechanical, including photocopying, recording, or by any information storage and retrieval system, without permission in writing from the publisher. All of the *Kit-Cat*® and Friends drawings are copyrighted and can be used only with written permission. Reviewers have permission to quote from this book.

Library of Congress   Cataloging-in-Publication Data
Toay, John B.
    So You've Been Asked To Pray

    Bibliography: p. 128
    1. Prayers. 2. Authors and publishers -
United States. I. Young, Woody C.
CIP: 90-62177

ISBN   0-939513-40-4

Kit-Cat drawings copyrighted 1990 Woody Young Creations.

KIT-CAT is a registered trademark of the California Clock Co. and is used with permission.

TABLE OF CONTENT

Preface

Introduction

How To Begin And End In Prayer

Salutations

Conclusions

14. Making The Ordinary Sacred
(Gratitude for the common things in life)

15. Facing The Grind
(How to overcome the monotonous)

16. The Proper Perspective
(How to simplify our lives)

17. Helping Humankind
(Good for brotherhood week)

18. Discovering Exhaustless Resources
(Teaching us how to pray)

19. The Ridiculous And The Sublime
(Seeking spiritual insight)

20. Each New Day
(Making today count)

21. Pausing For A Moment
(Asking for a new resolve; dedication)

22. Lift Us
(Teach us how to look at life)

23. Prayer Is Always Somewhere
(Brotherhood)

24. Leaders Of Vision
(How to make life easier)

25. Speeding On Life's Highway
(How to understand life's journey)

26. Let Us Become Children Again
(A prayer when families are involved)

27. For Families
(Family models in our day)

28. America, Love It And Change It
(How to understand dissent as loyalty)

29. Free The Prisoners
(A prayer for patriotism and freedom)

30. For Peace Of Mind
(A prayer seeking the peace of God)

31. Listening To Jiminy Cricket
(Prayer to hear the inner voice before action)

32. Is It Right?
(Prayer for right choices)

33. Transportation That Prevents Collisions
(Prayer on how we travel through life)

34. Decisions Are Not Easy
(Prayer for political groups)

35. Thanks For Friends That Care
(Recognizing special people in our lives)

36. The Right Position For Prayer
(Prayer for physical conference, YMCA)

37. For Those Who Wear Masks
(Prayer for mental health)

38. Working With People
(Prayer for installation of officers or first meeting)

39. Those Who Are Special To Children
(Prayer when children or families are involved)

40. Insert Foot, Wiggle Toes
(Teach us when to speak and what to say)

41. Teach Us What Freedom Is
(Patriotism and appreciating one another)

42. When A Great Tragedy Occurs
(Prayer for understanding and help)

43. Paying The Price
(Prayer for understanding how to achieve success)

44. Teach Us That Our Lives Are Important
(A call to commitment)

45. Making Today Count
(The importance of now)

46. Bifocals Of Faith
(Prayer for insight and new vision)

47. Our Responsibility For The World
(Prayer for trust; good for first meeting)

48. The Tyranny Of Trifles
(A prayer to set priorities)

49. Is It Popular Or Is It Right?
(Asking for understanding before action)

50. Teach Us True Discrimination
(Help us to understand what is real)

51. Playing Hide And Seek
(Prayer for honest living)

52. Just Repair Work
(Prayer For handling aging)

53. Thank You For Volunteers
(Prayer of appreciation for those who volunteer)

54. Riding On Tires That Need Deflating
(Asking for a faith-lift)

55. The Eyes Have It
(A prayer for looks that cure)

Prayers for Special Days

New Year	January 1
Lincoln's Birthday	February 12
Washington's Birthday	February 22
President's Day	3rd Monday/February
Easter	March/April
St. Patrick's Day	March 17
Mother's Day	2nd Sunday/May
Memorial Day	Last Monday/May
Flag Day	June 14
Independence Day	July 4
Labor Day	1st Monday/September
Halloween	October 31
National Elections	1st Tuesday after 1st Monday/Nov.
Christmas	December 25

Other Special Themes

Installation of Officers
The End of Summer
Funeral for a Friend
Labor/Management Dispute

DEDICATION

by Dr. John Toay

To my wife and best friend

Barbara

and

To one of her favorite cousins

Phil Stiles

who originated the idea for this book

by Woody Young

To the Knox Fellowship Team

my prayer partners

Prayer brings people together.

Preface

More than just a book on prayers, this book is intended to touch the heart. It is the heart which sets the mood. With that in mind, the *Kit-Cat*® sayings and cartoons may just be the catalyst you need to direct your mind towards the true meaning of prayer.

Before saying a prayer you might want to take a moment to reflect on what many have found to be the positive aspects of prayer. You may want to try sharing one of the prayer thoughts of the *Kit-Cat*® captions.

The authors, with years of public speaking experience, feel that with the help of this book's mood setting sayings and mind soothing prayers you can be excited about having been asked to give the tone setting prayer.

Woody Young

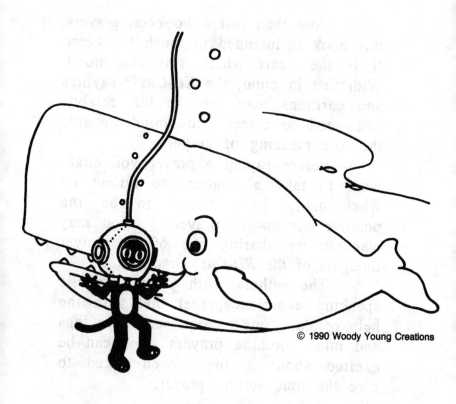

A prayer can make an introduction memorable!

Introduction

A speaker at a service club once said something I've never forgotten. "The only way to start a meeting with a bang is to use a gun or a cap pistol." There is another way. It isn't always recognized, but it is the reason for this little book. I believe that one of the most important events in any meeting is to consider, if only for a moment, that we are in the presence of God. We are God's creatures. Therefore, a prayer to begin any event can set the stage for whatever will happen. It can mean absolutely nothing or can be an acknowledgement that we are once again dependent upon Him who gives us every good and perfect gift. Thus, thanks is in order.

Often the attitude about convening a meeting with prayer is that it's a necessary formality. It is a traditional or ceremonial nuisance. But many men and women I've known over the years feel it is a meaningful moment to share with others gratitude to God, and a reminder of His goodness and grace.

Praying in public is not easy. There are many organizations that pass the job around. Some individuals are comfortable with the task, but many feel very inadequate. As a minister, I have done my share of praying at meetings and am pleased when someone else is asked to pray. I feel that I am often asked because it is an expected responsibility that goes with the territory. The attitude, "I'll do it in a pinch, but it is easier to be led than to lead," is one that we all understand.

Several years ago, my wife's cousin called me and needed a prayer. We discussed it and developed one over the telephone. He said, "Why don't we collaborate and write a book for people like me that are asked, but don't know what to say." I put the suggestion on the back burner, but finally decided that perhaps it would meet a real need. The result is **So You've Been Asked To Pray.**

I have been a Presbyterian minister for over thirty-five years. You have heard of church hopping. I've done my "hopping" with service clubs. I was a member of the Lions Club in Jesup, Iowa; the Optimist Club in San Diego, California; the Rotary Club in Niagara Falls, New York; and the Kiwanis Club in Downey, California. And I discovered that all of these fine organizations have one thing in common. They begin their meetings with prayer.

I work for a Commander-in-Chief who expects that there will be a certain amount of attention given to Him by all present when He is addressed. I don't think He is always impressed by the way our conversation with Him is handled. For those who take public prayer seriously then, it does become an awesome responsibility.

These prayers are meant to be catalysts for your use. They can be used just as they are written or as thoughts to inspire your own prayer. My hope is that they will be used to enhance your organization's sense of the importance of a moment with God as you begin your meeting.

Dr. John B. Toay

A warm prayer... glows like a bright star!

How To Begin And End In Prayer

Prayer is not a problem when in a mosque, synagogue, cathedral, or church because the people who are praying and those who are listening are like-minded in their faith journey. But there has been great concern on how to begin and conclude public prayers. This is because of the different attitudes and faiths of persons attending community and civic meetings. Because of this very important difference, we need to examine how we should pray in public.

To me, prayer needs to be exclusive and inclusive at the same time. When that is understood by the person praying aloud and the people who are listening and making it their prayer, there is absolutely no problem. But for persons who are either insensitive in leading a prayer or who are ready to criticize because the words are not what they expect, it can be a thorny issue.

This should cause us to question our attitude about how we pray in public. We should choose carefully our words when we are leading in public prayer. And we should allow the words to become our prayer when we are led by another person.

A prayer always needs to be personal, even when we are praying in public. Real communication with God is an I-Thou relationship before it can become a We-Thou relationship. For this reason we need to pray as naturally as we can in public, realizing that we are one nation under God and that it is in God we trust and that it is to our personal God we pray.

The greatest difficulty, I believe, is at the end of a prayer. This is most often true for the Christian who is praying aloud and for the non-Christian who is listening to the prayer. People who have asked me to pray in public have shared their concern about my concluding a prayer in Jesus' name. I have explained that as a Christian pastor, I always conclude my prayers in His name, whether I lead in prayer or am led in prayer by a person of any other faith.

In turn, I expect everyone who is there to be aware of his/her personal God and the unity in which we all approach Him.

If there are words that do not fit what I believe, I am not offended, but made more aware of the uniqueness of people and a Creator God who loves us all, sometimes because of what we say to Him, but most of the time in spite of what we say.

In my concluding words, I do not intend to exclude others and yet I do want to be faithful to the God whom I believe is revealed in Jesus Christ. I do not expect the non-Christian to conclude his or her prayer in the same way I would, nor do I feel excluded from that prayer. That makes prayer, for me, exclusive and inclusive at the same time in every situation.

Prayer, then, is personally exclusive for each of us, but we need to feel included and to include others in every public prayer we offer, moving beyond the words to the Word. Prayers are not meant to be used as tools or excuses to promote one's own theological bias. They are meant to be real communication shared between God and His people.

The following are some exclusive and inclusive salutations and conclusions that should be understood as personal but corporately meaningful by all persons, regardless of their faith. These are only examples and should not be considered, even remotely, a complete list. You can use many others that are probably better suited for the way you want to pray in an exclusive, inclusive manner. In this book I have not used either salutation or conclusion in the prayers. You may select one of the following or use your own. Just be thoughtful of your audience and by that I mean your God.

Inclusive and Exclusive Salutations

"Our Gracious, Loving and Everpresent God"

"O God, our Help in ages past, our Hope for years to come"

"O God of our Fathers and Mothers, of Abraham and Sarah, of Isaac and Rebecca, of Jacob, Rachel and Leah, and Our God"

"O Creator, Redeemer, and Sustainer in Life"

"Our Sovereign King"

"O Lord God"

"To the One God, Whom we give glory and honor"

"O God, our God"

Exclusive and Inclusive Conclusions

"In the name of Him who holds us in His hand and who loves us with an everlasting love, Amen"

"In His Holy Name we pray, Amen"

"And now, O God, may we all feel included as we pray this prayer in the name of the one whom we call God, Amen"

"In the name of Jesus, who many of us call Lord, and who all of us acknowledge as a man who went about doing good, Amen"

"And even as Jesus increased in wisdom and stature and in favor with God and man, may that be our goal for growth day by day, Amen"

"May our prayer be heard, O God, because we trust in you and believe, Amen"

A prayer is a simple step to better communication!

For Service Organizations

1

Prayer Is Conversation

Help us today to see our opening prayer as conversation, really believing You hear us and care about what we say.

Remind us that You are a perfect Father who listens carefully to His children and desires the very best for us.

We thank You for this family of(Kiwanis or Rotary or Optomist, etc.) to which we belong and ask that You bless us as we meet together.

An Audience With The King

It is so easy for prayer to become for us a necessary preliminary to a meeting--something we too easily take for granted.

Startle us into realizing that we are beginning this meeting with an audience before the King of Kings. As your subjects, we ask You to honor us with Your blessing as we meet together.

The next time you want to feel better... pray!

3

Grateful   Praise

"For the beauty of the earth,
For the glory of the skies,
For Your love which from our birth
over and around us lies,
Lord of all, to Thee we raise
this our prayer of grateful praise."

Praying keeps you feeling wonderful!

Fun, Inspiration, And Fellowship

We are meeting today for some fun and possibly some inspiration and certainly some fellowship. These three parts of life we accept so easily.

But today give us a sense that these are unique to the human spirit. Created in Your image, we have been given a sense of humor. Created as Your children, we have the ability to soar in spirit. And created as a part of the human family, we relish the times of comradeship with other friends.

May each of these--fun, inspiration, and fellowship--take place in our meeting today.

© 1990 Woody Young Creations

A prayer gives you a God-backed guarantee.

Our Roots In God's Love

The apostle Paul once prayed that "our roots might go deep down into the soil of God's marvelous love....until we are filled up with God himself." Often our roots are strangled by the busyness of life and the worries that surround us.

Send Your refreshing, life-giving water up from the depths of the earth, to expand and explode those roots with new life so that we each can blossom and bear fruit in all that we do.

God's Guarantee

We thank You that as a guarantee of Your presence, You have promised us Your Spirit. In that Spirit, we thank You today for the full and rich life within each of us.

Breathe on us, breath of God. Fill us with life anew, that we may live as Thou dost live, and do as Thou wouldst do.

Quiet Us

It is not easy in a loud and noisy world to stop and be quiet, even for a moment.

Sometimes stillness and silence can be disturbing. But there are times, O God, when silence can be so meaningful and refreshing.

And so we pray that You will quiet us, and speak to us today in the silence of this moment. It was out of the silence that You spoke and the world was created. So, at this time, it is in the silence that You can speak and our spirits can be revived.

Help us to hear Your words, "be still and know that I am God" and in the stillness discover what that really means.

© 1990 Woody Young Creations

Pray and put your worries to rest.

Waiting Upon God

We know that it is good to take a moment to "wait upon You." You have such great promises for us if we do. As Isaiah prophesied, "Those who wait upon the Lord shall renew their strength. They shall mount up with wings as eagles. They shall run and not be weary. They shall walk and not faint."

It would be exhilerating to fly. For the joggers in our group, it is great to run. But for most of us, it is enough to be able to walk through today without becoming fainthearted.

Whatever mood we are in, help us to wait upon You and receive Your blessing so that we can at least walk, and perhaps run the race that You have set before us with new vigor and hope.

And we dare to ask for the courage to fly, to dream new dreams and to let our minds soar. Bless us as an organization and as individuals as we "wait upon You."

Your prayer is as unique as you are!

We're All Different

It is good to recognize how different we are, O God. Our talents, our dreams, our backgrounds, our occupations. And it is good to know that when You created each of us, You broke the mold. No one is exactly like anyone else. Even our thumb print and our voice track tell us how unique we are.

Yet, we thank You that we can take these differences and mobilize them for the good of (Jaycees/etc.) and our community.

In our differences we can think the same thoughts and move together toward a common goal. Bless us as we meet together.

Thank You for our individuality and also for our common bond.

Colors In Life

A rainbow in the sky excites us, O God, because of the promise of your love that it represents. And the magnificent colors in it often express the best and the worst in our lives.

Save us today from being green with envy or jealousy, or blue and depressed, or yellow and cowardly in our decisions and attitudes in life, or flushed red with anger.

May we be strong, bright, and lively, rather than pastel and bland. And may others look at the brush strokes of our deeds and see vividly the pictures we are drawing through our actions as individuals and as a club.

Blend the colors of our lives into a rainbow of promise.

Praying As Children

An easy prayer we learned as children was "Now I lay me down to sleep" and a camp prayer for meals was "Rub a dub, dub; thanks for the grub."

Although these are prayers learned by kids, and we feel uncomfortable or amused by them, they do convey a wonderful thought that we should never forget.

Every good and perfect gift comes from You, O God, and we need to be reminded of that over and over again.

And so we take time to thank You for life in its abundance, for the food we eat and those with whom we eat it, and for the promise of Your presence with us, both now and forever.

A prayer can help brighten even the cloudiest of days!

Mountaintop Or Valley?

Some of us are on a mountaintop today looking at life with enthusiasm and vitality, waiting for the next great thing to happen. Others of us are in the valley of despair wondering when the next load will be dropped and we feel like that cartoon character who always has it raining only on him.

When we look honestly at life, our God, we know that nothing can stop either the good or the bad from changing. And so, help us, whatever our mood may be, to understand that simple truth.

May we enjoy the blessings that we experience. May we also be given strength to endure the difficulties we face.

Help each of us to become sensitive to the needs of one another in both joys and sorrows. And no matter what our mood, may we be very aware of Your presence and consistent love.

© 1990 Woody Young Creations

A prayer changes how you feel about life!

Thank You !

Listen to our hearts, dear Lord,
and let these two words say it all--
Thank You.

Making The Ordinary Sacred

In this quiet moment help us to understand that everything we have is a gift from You and that You make the common things in life sacred.

We thank You for those things we take for granted; the land we stand upon, the air we breath, the food we eat and the water we drink and swim in. We thank You for schools, for jobs, for skills, for routines and surprises, for entertainment, for something to do and for time off for each other.

Remind us that nothing is ordinary; that everything given for our need is a special gift from our extraordinary God.

15

Facing The Grind

This is the common prayer we make, asking You to help us face the grind of the monotonous and the humdrum routine of duty with a new vision.

May our faith have feet and hands, a voice and a heart, that we may give to others in the common things of life. May our faith shine in our faces and be seen in our lives.

© 1990 Woody Young Creations

Want to start improving your life...
try praying!

The Proper Perspective

Help us to realize that we should never fall in love with things. Help us to understand that our life today is a journey, a pilgrimage, a training school for a wonderful future.

Then we shall have the proper perspective. Then we shall fall in love with the things that endure beyond time and space. Give us the courage to simplify our lives.

So may we be mature in our faith; childlike, but never childish, humble, but never cringing, understanding, but never conceited.

So help us to live and not merely exist.

Helping Humankind

Today we pray that we may receive Your special blessing because we are committed to be a real service organization to help humankind.

May each of us in our daily routine come to know the joy of caring and sharing with others not as fortunate as we are.

May our motto that includes caring and sharing be for us life service as well as lip service.

Discovering Exhaustless Resources

There are times when our hearts almost burst from gratitude and joy. We can't understand it, but we feel trapped inside.

There is something shouting to get out. Could it be the spirit that You have planted in each one of us?

Teach us that to pray is to be a partner with You. Teach us that to pray is to gain access to the exhaustless resources which You have for us.

We thank You that in this moment You have linked us to Yourself through prayer.

The Ridiculous And The Sublime

When we pray we move from the ridiculous to the sublime. In reality we do not leave the presence of one another and we do not enter into Your presence. But in the spiritual realm that is exactly what we do.

Will You help us shut out the noises of this world, so we can hear Your voice? Give us an insight to behold new vistas of opportunity and challenge that comes from You?

Then give us the ability to share. In that way, O God, help us move back from the sublime to the ridiculous, from Your presence into the presence of one another.

Each New Day

Each day is a new day. This is a simple but profound truth. And each day brings discouragements. We know that is a part of life, but it is hard to take.

Fullfill Your promise to be with us particularly during discouraging times. Give us vision to see the good in the bad, Your purposes hidden in the present circumstances. May the difficulties become stepping stones rather than stumbling blocks.

And each day brings choices and decisions to be made. Grant us wisdom to see the right and the wrong. Help us to walk a path that is pleasing to You.

Father, strengthen our faith and increase our love, today and in all the todays that begin tomorrow.

© 1990 Woody Young Creations

A prayer says there's a spirit of cooperation!

Pausing For A Moment

We pause for a moment from the busy life we lead. We have determined to be a part of a service organization that assists our community.

We who are specks of dust on a small planet that is spinning around in the vast expanse of space, dare to say that we offer ourselves to You, the great Creator of this earth, and the solar system, and galaxy, and universe. What need do You have of our service?

Yet You have shared with us that though we are but fragile bits of dust whose days are few, we are meant to have eternal and abiding purposes for living.

Give us that sense of worth, of value, of meaning that emboldens us to be better than we could be on our own....to be more loving than we could be without You....and to have the humility to hear You say, "Whom shall I send?".... and the courage to respond, "Here am I, Lord. Use me."

Lift Us

Today we ask You to lift us up so that all that is excellent rises like the morning sun upon the earth.

Lift us from ingratitude to thankfulness. Our life is mingled with things both good and bad, happy and unhappy. Our fortunes are inconsistent. Forgive our eyes their tendency to center only on the dark side. Forgive our imaginations that see only monsters.

Help us to see the good and that the monsters are only shadows created by our fears. Give us the inner certainty of faith to know that You are in control and that all things, even in this moment, are working together for good because we trust in You.

O God, lift us from ingratitude to thankfulness.

Prayer Is Always Somewhere

We lift up our voices in this moment to join the chorus of prayer that is never silent. As day follows night, so over all the continents of the earth, always at any moment there is someone joining in prayer and praise to You.

May our prayer be a link of faith in an endless and unbreakable chain binding us to You and to one another.

O God of everywhere, give us keen eyes to recognize You in our homes, at work, everywhere we go.

Help us to really understand that it is in You that we live and move and have our being! Be a living presence to us here and now.

© 1990 Woody Young Creations

Only when you pray can you be the best you can be!

Leaders Of Vision

We pray today for vision. So often it is the blind leading the blind. We pray for insight so we can see at least a little way ahead and know what we ought to do. In our personal lives make our paths plainer until problems grow less complex and duties more clear.

Grant us, O God, great vision to our inner eyes. Help us so that our perspectives do not become too narrow. We pray for eternal horizons around our daily duties.

Lift us to such an altitude that we may open our eyes after this prayer and look at our world as new men and women.

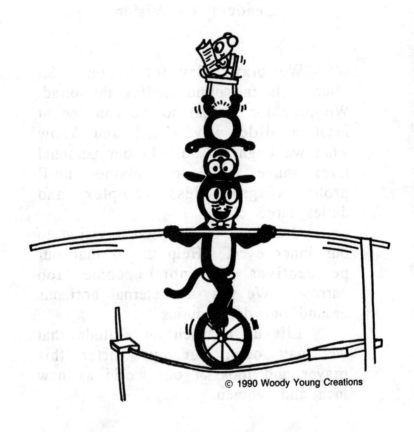

© 1990 Woody Young Creations

Praying keeps your life in balance!

Speeding On Life's Highway

Forgive us, our God, for not obeying the speed laws in life that You have set for us. Help us to obey the colors of the lights and go when they are green and stop when they are red.

When refreshed in spirit, may nothing stop us, but when we need to take time to pull into a rest stop, help us to do just that.

Praying is something you never outgrow.

Let Us Become Children Again

It's fun to have fun. We recognize, our God, that we have forgotten what it is to be like children, playing games for the sake of playing games. We have lost our childhood too easily. We pray for the ability to become childlike again.

Help us to become inquisitive and ask all the "why" questions like we used to. Help us to discover the priority of having some good friends and best friends. Help us to feel time as it used to feel....slow and steady.

Give us adventures that cause us to dare risking and ideas that we are not afraid to tackle. Allow us to fight the dragons and win and to save the maidens in distress.

O God, as our Heavenly father, help us once in a while to dream dreams and see visions and become children again.

For Families

We thank You for placing some of us in families where we have been nurtured and loved. And we thank You for leading others of us to this time and place, caring for us in spite of our family background and lack of love.

We ask a blessing upon those in unique families who need Your special favors; upon single parents and their children; upon men and women who have lost their partners; upon those who are older and were a part of a large family but are now the last and alone; upon children who have never been loved and in their innocence are even now in danger.

And we pray for the families that we represent. May our families become what You desire and may we be responsible to see that it happens.

America, Love It And Change It

At times we have heard someone say, "America, love it or leave it." Help us, O God, to love it for its best and to change it from its worst. Renew our respect for one another and for the diversity that makes us great.

May we never confuse dissent with disloyalty in our love for this great land of opportunity and freedom.

May we mold our vision into realities as our alabaster cities become undimmed by human tears. "America, America, God shed His grace on thee, and crown Thy good with brotherhood, from sea to shining sea."

let us live to make men free,

Free The Prisoners

Too often, Our God, we think of prisoners being those captives confined to jails. Today we acknowledge that many of us are in prisons of our own making.

We are captives of habits that make us less than we should be. Some of us are bound by the ropes of moral weakness or physical illness who long for the freedom of health. Some of us are prisoners of loneliness, longing for the chains to be broken by friendship.

We also remember the people of other nations who have had their freedoms stolen.

May these prisoners of human tyranny discover from You a flame of freedom that never dies out.

Today may each of us discover the wonderful promises of liberty that are ours as the children of God.

Praying brings out the best in all of us.

© 1990 Woody Young Creations

For Peace Of Mind

We know that the only way to peace in this world or in our minds is from and through You.

We begin life full of needs and the needs continue. And the turmoil in our lives all come from trying to meet those needs with the wrong things, in the wrong places, at the wrong time.

Help us to stop fixing what doesn't need it. May we not look for trouble, because we know that when we don't find it, we often start it.

Give us that peace that passes all human understanding, knowing that it is from You and that it comes with no regrets.

Listening To Jiminy Cricket

Isaiah once predicted that our ears will hear a voice behind us, saying, "This is the way, walk in it, and do not turn aside." (Isaiah 30:21)

It is not in the rustling grass that we hear You pass, but in the still, small voice of conscience. Give each of us a Jiminy Cricket that chirps so loud there will be no indecision in our attitudes or our actions.

And may that inner voice become a thunderous roar if we fail to hear and to heed the direction You want us to take. We pray for this in our individual lives and in the life of our fellowship.

Is It Right?

When we begin something and are not sure what to do, in our choices let us not ask, "Will it work?" but, rather, "Is it right?"

When we seek Your blessing, remind us that we cannot fool You, though we may be fooling ourselves.

Remind us that as we devise our own plans and then have the nerve to ask You to bless them, that there are some things You cannot and will not bless. And unless Your blessing is upon what we do, we are wasting our time.

So guide us to ask from the beginning, "Is it right?", and then to hear Your answer before we begin. Then, O God, bless us in our endeavor.

© 1990 Woody Young Creations

Take a chance... pray!

Transportation That Prevents Collisions

When we travel down life's highway we like to use different kinds of transportation depending on our determined destinations of the moment. When we are anxious to get somewhere we are ready to use the jet plane. When we have an appointment we would rather not keep, the covered wagon would be the best way to go.

But, then, most of us find ourselves just going along for the ride and not being able to get into the driver's seat.

Help us to fashion our journey each day with the mode You have designed for us, and make us sensitive to our fellow travelers. In that way may we prevent collisions and arrive safely where You want us to be.

© 1990 Woody Young Creations

When you consider the alternatives, opt for praying!

Decisions Are Not Easy

Martin Luther once mentioned that we should "Trust God and sin bravely." And we recognize that is not easy to do. It gives us freedom that can be dangerous and opportunity that we can abuse. We have to make decisions when sometimes there are not black and white answers. Yet we have to make choices and no decision is not an option.

Will You be with us when we decide? Let our choices be born out of total trust in Your guidance. Then, when the decision is made, give us the power to recognize Your hand in it.

A prayer is the shortest distance between two people.

Thanks For Friends That Care

We thank You for all those who love us and for those good friends who let us know they care by a winsome smile, a firm handshake, a bear hug. We thank You for unexpected phone calls and long letters and short notes. We thank You for everything that others do to help us understand that we are important to them.

In this fellowship we thank You for those who have gone the second mile, but also for those who have just gone the first and by carrying our burden for a moment, have made our individual loads easier.

Bind us together into a fellowship of love......and in our pains and pleasures, help us to be good to and for one another.

© 1990 Woody Young Creations

Praying... recommended by happy people everywhere!

The Right Position For Prayer

What is the right position for prayer? Should we be in a closet on our knees with our eyes closed or can we pray confidently in a large gathering standing up with our eyes wide open? Help us to understand that the places and physical positions are not important, but that the spiritual postures are central.

As we pray today, may our prayers come through loud and clear because our spiritual knees are bent, our hearts are open, and our eyes are upon You. May we then stand tall, knowing that we have been heard.

© 1990 Woody Young Creations

Praying brings out the best in you.

For Those Who Wear Masks

We all wear masks at times to fool people. Lord, we know that we cannot fool You. Help us to be more honest with others. Some of us act like we don't need people, but we understand that "people who need people are the luckiest people in the world", so we pray for those who don't seem to need others.

Some of us are laughing on the outside while we cry in anguish or for help on the inside. Bless us with someone who can be trusted to laugh with us and also cry with us.

Some of us act so cold at times and you know that it is our shyness that comes across as being too good for others and unfriendly. Yet we want friends desperately. Give us the courage to discover how great it feels to take off the masks and be as real to others as we are to You.

Working With People

There are three words that describe both the advantages and disadvantages of every job and organization in which we work or belong--working with people.

Why is it, Lord, that some people can be so wonderful and some just the opposite? It's just a thought, but could it be possible that each of us fits both of these catagories in our relationships to other people?

Give us the ability to see ourselves as others see us, and to take the giant redwood out of our own eye before we point the finger at the toothpick dangling from our neighbors. And give us the power to work with others demonstrating the same kind of love that we would expect.

May the golden rule, "do unto others as you would have them do unto you," be our guideline.

Those Who Are Special To Children

We thank You for all of those who are special to children. We thank You for the story tellers, the clowns, the people who sell ice cream and candy and toys and all the things children love, special teachers who really care about young people and their growth of knowledge and life, pediatricians who often scare but also care, the Muppets and Dr. Suess and all of the other entertainers who over the years have touched children's interests in so many special ways.

We thank You for those who are willing to take on projects to help the youth of our community and give of themselves through their hours of service and their financial contributions. We thank You that our organization has played a part in helping children laugh and learn and love. We thank You, O God, for all who are special to children.

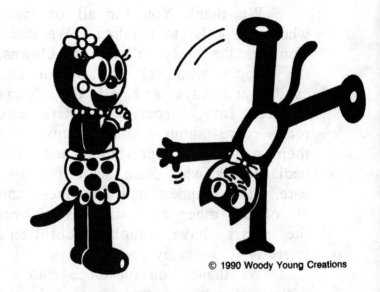

© 1990 Woody Young Creations

**A prayer gives personality to the words...
I love you!**

Insert Foot, Wiggle Toes

None of us can escape putting our foot in our mouth at times and some of us, our God, have the unique capacity of wiggling our toes once we insert the foot. Today we would ask for help in thinking before we speak and in cultivating proper speech. We are surrounded by men and women in our community who are able to use stirring words to inspire and encourage and transform. May we learn to say what we mean and mean what we say. And may it be worth saying.

Give us guidance to speak so that we will not easily wound or offend with our words. In what we say, may we produce light without generating heat. We know that if we bridle our tongues there can't be enough room left for our feet as well. Teach us and then remind us constantly what to say and how to say it.

Teach Us What Freedom Is

We pray today for all of the people in our country. Red and yellow, black and white, we are all precious in Your sight. Thus in our uniqueness of heritage and personality we are also bound together by Your love. We thank You that You love each of us and all of us. Help us to learn to appreciate one another.

We thank You for the goodly heritage that is ours. We need to learn, in these challenging days, that to every right there is attached a duty and to every privilege an obligation. Teach us, our God, what freedom is. May we all learn the lesson that it is not our right to do as we please, but our opportunity to please as we do what is right.

Most of all, help us never to forget that where Your Spirit is, there is freedom. May we discover the freedom that is ours because You are with us.

When A Great Tragedy Occurs

We pray that Your spirit will come into our hearts and make us sensitive to the sufferings of other people. We are mindful of those victims of the ravaging flood waters (or other mishap) and all those who have heavy hearts today. Bless each suffering person and family with a sense of Your presence and Your love. May those helpers who are able, move swiftly to rescue those in need.

Help us to grow in awareness and understanding so that the very sympathy we have for family and friends may also be felt for strangers. Then, O God, give us the opportunity in some way to show visibly how much we care.

Paying The Price

Help us to understand that there is a cost for everything. The best things in life are not free. Even Your love for us cost You a great price and our love for others demands sacrifice on our part.

We are reminded that the price for inner peace is our willingness to recognize our need to be forgiven. We pray for the awareness of our need and ask You to forgive us. May we have that peace that passes all human understanding and pay the price by sharing it with others.

May we pay the price of putting to death all of those things in our lives that would destroy, so that we might bring into our lives all of those things that would enhance and give life the meaning You have planned for us.

Help us to realize that without real effort there can be no accomplishment; without hard work there can be no achievement; and without Your help there can be no success or victory.

Teach Us That Our Lives Are Important

Some of us feel that our thoughts are not often great and never original. Some of us had planned on better or at least different occupations than we now have. Some of us are wondering what happened to the dream of a happy marriage or proud parenthood that we had. Some of us are ready to stop the world so we can get off.

Teach us, our God, that we all have problems of one kind or another and when solutions do not come easily, our reaction becomes one of frustration and a sense of hopelessness and with that comes the feeling of insignificance. Who am I? No one, really! What can I do? Nothing, really!

Then remind us that You are always here for us, that we are each part of Your great plan and that the most important thing we can do is trust You. Help us move from the problems we face to the solution You will give. Help us to do the one thing that we can do and that is "Let Go and Let God."

© 1990 Woody Young Creations

Pray, because you've got a lot of living to do!

Making Today Count

How often have we heard that today is the beginning of the rest of our lives? Yesterday is memory; tomorrow is hope; today is the only reality that there really is.

Our God, help us to realize how much truth there is in these statements so that we can make this very moment in which we are living and breathing special. May we each make the "here and now" count for something.

Teach us to use each moment wisely, even if we are unable to see its eternal effect. Teach us to handle the tasks of today, whether easy or difficult, for they are gifts that we should not squander before time takes them from us. Teach us not to neglect this minute, for it will never come again.

O God, help us to make today count!

© 1990 Woody Young Creations

***Even the world's smallest prayer can have a
big impact!***

Bifocals Of Faith

It is so easy on rainy days to forget that beyond the clouds the sun is shining brightly. And it is easy in life, when the sky is dark and uncertain to forget that goodness and rightness will untimately prevail.

We pray, our God, for the bifocals of faith so that we can see the concern of the moment right under our noses, but also see, further on, Your purpose in working out Your plan in the world You have made.

We pray for the ability to see at close range our part as a group to become solution partners in the giving of time and effort and money, and we pray also for the ability to see clearly in the distance, those who are in partnership with us.

May we look with new vision through these bifocals of faith and then act.

Our Responsibility For The World

In the face of life's mysteries and the vast universe filled with galaxies beyond our imagination, help us to believe that You are not only the creator of all, but continue to work through us to complete Your creation.

You have commanded us to be stewards of the world in which we live. You have given us not only the opportunity to have dominion over the earth but also the responsibility to care for it and keep it.

Strengthen our conviction that Your hand is upon us, to lead us and to use us in working out Your purposes in the world, beginning with our own organization.

And even though we may not see the distant scene, give us the ability to take one step at a time and trust You for the rest.

The Tyranny Of Trifles

This is the day You have made. Help us to be filled with gratitude and find joy in it. May we appreciate its beauty and use its opportunities fully. In order to do that we need to be delivered from the tyranny of trifles.

Help us to give our best thoughts to what is important, so that what we accomplish will be worth while. Give us the spiritual ears to hear the prompting of Your spirit and then be spared from indecisions that waste time, subtract from our vision and goal, divide our efficiency and multiply our troubles.

© 1990 Woody Young Creations

A prayer... bears your personal certificate of authenticity!

Is It Popular Or Is It Right?

So often, our God, we differ in approaches to life and also to problems we face. This should seem natural because we are all different and look differently at situations.

But strangely, even when we admit this, it is hard to accept someone else's solution if it is not like ours. Help us to be open to one another and to at least consider another way. It might even be a better way. May we always be guided, not by whether it is popular, or expedient, or practical, but always by whether it is right.

Guide us as individuals and as a club to be led by what we know to be right.

Teach Us True Discrimination

Teach us true discrimination, our God.

We need to be able to tell the difference between faith and fatalism, between activity and accomplishment, between humility and an inferiority complex, between a quick salute to You and a real prayer that seeks to find out Your will.

Our God, teach us true discrimination.

Playing Hide And Seek

We spend a lot of time in life playing hide-and-seek. We play the game with our business associates, with our friends, with our families and loved ones and with You. It is so much easier at times to hide than to be discovered. And it is so much easier to play games than to deal with life.

But You've caught us and we can't keep playing the game because we are now "it." Others may still be trying to find us. Others may still be trying to discover the real me. But You didn't have any trouble and now we can't play the game anymore. Now we have to show ourselves as we really are, particularly to others who are trying to stop playing the game.

But what a relief. Now we can be honestly ourselves to You and to others. No more dishonest games. Only honest living. What a relief. Thank you, God.

Pray and invite God to be your friend.

52
Just Repair Work

I receive a birthday card that explains that from now on, in life, it is all just repair work. I don't feel any older than my grandchildren and yet, chronologically, I have passed the half-century mark and then some. Why does age make such a difference when I feel so young in body, as well as mind and spirit?

I know some people that act aged in their teens and some in their eighties who would fit into the "rock generation" easily and comfortably. What makes the difference, Lord? You have given us the answer. It is a matter of the heart. As a person thinks in his heart, so is he!

The youthful spirit belongs to all of us if we will have it. From our birth, there is repair work to be done. But until the end there is enthusiasm, joy, faith, hope, and love to be had and shared by all of us, no matter what our age.

Someone has said, "Live each day as if it were your last, but plan to live forever, because both statements are true." Lord, make our lives more than just repair work.

Thank You For Volunteers

Thank you, God, for volunteers. Where would the world be without those who are willing to give of their effort and effects, of their time and talents and money to meet the needs of this community, this nation, and this world.

We thank You for the many reasons people give when they are asked why they volunteer. Some do it out of love for You. Some do it because they see a great need. Some do it because other friends are doing it and its fun to do it together.

Our God, it is interesting that the word, "volunteer," has behind it the thought that someone is doing something for nothing which could not be farther from the truth. There is a sense of satisfaction of doing good and that is the gift received. Most volunteers wouldn't, if there would not be the satisfaction of a job well done. Thank You, God, for volunteers and the satisfactions they receive.

Riding On Tires That Need Deflating

We feel good when as a group or as persons we learn something. We seem, however, to make such little progress in our spiritual growth, and for this, O God, we are sorry.

We have been riding comfortably on the round tires of conceit. For our own good we may have to be deflated, so that on the rims of humility, we may find those spiritual precepts that allow us to grow in our faith.

If our pride has to be punctured, we would pray that it will be done quickly, before we gain too much speed and have a tremendous wreck that is beyond repair.

Lord, help us to let You drive. We really need to learn to ride with You before we take the wheel.

© 1990 Woody Young Creations

A prayer helps you capture a renewed spirit!

The Eyes Have It

There are all kinds of looks, Lord. There are those that can kill but there are also those that are filled with love that can cure hurt and hate. There are stares that can cause wars and loving looks that can destroy prejudice.

There are "dirty looks," "scornful looks," "unbelieving looks," looks that can stop you in your tracks, and looks that can melt your heart and cause you to tremble in love. Give to us the ability to have the look that can cure, not kill.

A prayer from the past can make a perfect present!

Prayers for Special Days

NEW YEAR
[January 1]

Today we feel like either a new baby or an old man. Few of us feel we are in the middle. The year is over, yet for some of us it is still here, and we can't seem to shake the shadows of the past. The new year is beginning, yet for some of us the future is dark and mysterious and we feel uncomfortable about that.

The book of last year is really closed and the new year is opened with fresh pages upon which to write. God, help us to write our story, filled with faith and hope and love as we move into this new year.

LINCOLN'S BIRTHDAY
[February 12]

Abraham Lincoln once said that people are about as happy as they make up their minds to be and that everyone over forty is responsible for his own face. Lincoln was a man troubled by personal frictions and factions and misunderstandings all of his life and finally was faced with a war he did not want.

Sometimes we forget that our sixteenth President was a man who had a deep faith and a strong sense of humor to overcome and withstand overwhelming pressures. We pray for such men today and ask that the qualities in his life might be the goals for which we aim.

WASHINGTON'S BIRTHDAY
also called
President's Day
[February 22 or the 3rd Monday in February]

Chopping down the cherry tree, wooden false teeth, and a winter's ride across the Delaware without a seatbelt, standing precariously with one foot upon the bow of a rowboat, are all images we have of our first President.

But, our God, we pray that we might go beyond those pictures to see a man who truly was the father of our country. For his leadership, for his steadfastness, for his courage, and yes, for his honesty, we give You thanks.

For the forging of a nation and for the leading of an undisciplined people at our nation's beginning, we thank You for George Washington. May his ideals and ideas continue to be clear to the people of our day and may each of us embrace them and live by them.

© 1990 Woody Young Creations

Prayer... A gift from God!

EASTER

Easter is a time when we are not ashamed to admit that one of the greatest promises ever made was to give to each of us the gift of life that lasts forever. We thank You, O God, for life and the promise of life everlasting.

Squeezed in our mother's womb forever without birth is like being bound to this earth without the capacity to move beyond life to a freedom that transcends our greatest hopes or desires. You have given us the ability to have our heads in the clouds, even though now we must stand with our feet on the ground. Make Easter real to each of us today.

St. Patrick's Day
[March 17]

St. Patrick, in his autobiography from earliest British literature, wrote, "In a single day I said as many as a hundred prayers." This is a portion of one of them.

"I bind unto myself today
The power of God to hold and lead,
His eye to watch, His might to stay,
His ear to hearken to my need.
The wisdom of my God to teach,
His hand to guide, His shield to ward;
The word of God to give me speech,
His heavenly host to be my guard."

Although almost 1600 years separate us, may this prayer be our prayer for the day.

MOTHER'S DAY
[2nd Sunday in May]
[First observed in Philadelphia in
1908]

On this Mother's Day, receive our thanksgiving for every mother's love and care, in scrubbing hands and necks of little children and in wiping up misguided crayon marks on the wall.....in putting up with temper tantrums and in knowing when enough is enough....in preparing meals and knowing when to buy the hamburger or hotdog or taco.....in standing by her children when they need it and standing by the teacher or other authority when they need it.....in the thousand acts of love and caring each day.

If our mother is alive, we say a special prayer of thanksgiving for her and if our mother is no longer with us, we say a special prayer of gratitude for her.

MEMORIAL DAY
[Last Monday in May]
Also called
Decoration Day

Today we pray for the millions of soldiers and sailors over the years who have been enlisted in the service of their country. They have fought for the land they love in wars not of their making.

We pray for those maimed and handicapped by injuries to body and mind. We pray for the parents and the widows and the children whose loved ones died in battle. May not one who has given a life be forgotten. Let the hard lessons of war spur on our national and world leaders to discover ways for us to walk in the path of peace. Be with them in their hard decisions and with us in our valid support.

FLAG DAY
[June 14]

Our flag has grown from thirteen stars to fifty, with surely more stars to be placed in the future. When Betsy Ross began sewing that first symbol of our nation in the red, white and blue, little did she know what it would become.

Looking into the past, its symbolism is awesome. Looking into the future, only dreamers can really see what it will represent. We pray in gratitude for our past and our future, and pledge again our allegiance to the flag of the United States of America and to the republic for which it stands. May we truly be one nation, under God, with liberty and justice for all.

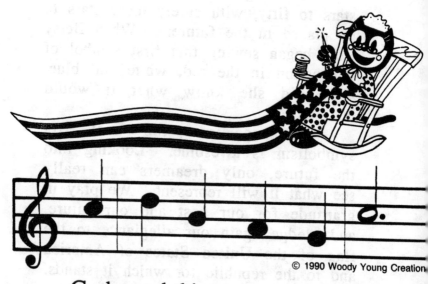

God mend thine ev- ery flaw,

INDEPENDENCE DAY
[July 4]

Freedom is a word that continues to ring as a loud bell around the world. We all want to be free. Help us to see, however, that all freedom demands responsibility; that to be independent, there is a dependence involved.

May we be dependent upon You, upon the law that gives us freedom within limits, and upon one another as we share both the opportunities and responsibilities of our independence. Lord, make us captives to this understanding and then we shall be free.

Three steps to better praying; practice, practice, practice!

LABOR DAY
[First Monday in September]

We pray today for the men and women who love their work and also for those who would like to change their jobs. Knowing the hours and weeks and years that go into our labors, may each of us discover that if we can't stand it, we'd better change it. And, our God, if we can't change it, give us the heart to be able to stand it.

Above all, give us a sense of satisfaction in our lives and in our relationships that go beyond our work-a-day world. Help us never to presume that we can work out the course of our lives separated from Your loving guidance and support. Bless us in life and in what we do.

LABOR DAY

"This is the gospel of labor,
Ring it, ye bells of the Kirk (church),
The Lord of love came down from
above
To live with the men who work.

This is the rose that he planted,
Here in our thorn-cursed soil.
The blessing of heaven is heavenly
rest,
But the blessing of earth is toil"

Help us to believe this and to
love our work.

HALLOWEEN
[October 31]

When we think of Halloween we see pumpkins, ghosts, little children going door to door with masks and costumes shouting "trick or treat," but we also are aware of some who are sick of mind, looking for unsuspecting victims to hurt or to rob. This season seems to bring out the best and the worst in us.

There are the razor blades and needles in apples, and there are the generous folk who have very little, but are willing to share what they have with eager, enthusiastic children. We pray today for the safety of our little ones and thank You for the generosity of our senior citizens. May this Halloween be both safe and sane.

© 1990 Woody Young Creations

Praying is the right choice!

ELECTION FOR CITY, STATE, NATION
[1st Tuesday after the 1st Monday in November]

We have voted or are about to vote today for the leaders of our city, state, and nation. Grant wisdom and good judgment to those men and women elected to serve us in civil leadership. May they be honest people who really are concerned for the welfare of Your people as one nation under God.

Give us the ability to be supportive as we see our leaders seeking our common good and Your grace.

© 1990 Woody Young Creations

Give the world a special gift... your prayer!

CHRISTMAS
[December 25]

As we hear the bells on Christmas Day ringing again from the church cathedrals and small village towers and in our heart of hearts, prepare us to find in Bethlehem Your promise of peace and joy and love.

This is a time of memories past, of family gatherings and love shared. And it is a time of present joy with thoughts of shepherds and wise men, and gifts given and received.

We thank You for the special gift of Yourself that we celebrate this season, for we are aware that the very word, Christmas, has Your name in it. And it is in that name of Love we give You thanks.

A prayer when you need it — is priceless!

INSTALLATION OF OFFICERS

This is the beginning of a new year for us, our God. May it be a good year, a productive year. Bless _____ as our new president, and those installed as officers. May each of us take an active part in leadership and in support so that our goals will be accomplished. Give us a strong sense of loyalty to (Rotary/etc.) and may that attitude be seen in every meeting we attend.

A prayer makes sure God gets the message!

THE END OF SUMMER

Back to school. Family reunions enjoyed. Vacations taken. New adventures and memories of summer past. Visits and barbecues close at hand and countries and sights never before seen long distances from here. Visitors received and relatives visited. Fellowship shared.

All these, O God, and more tell us that summer is over. We thank You for bringing us through our experiences to these days rested and refreshed. May this summer for each of us have been a time to prepare us to meet the challenges of the days ahead.

© 1990 Woody Young Creations

A prayer says, you have faith in God!

FUNERAL FOR A FRIEND

Even in the presence of the death of our friend, _____, our first word is a prayer of thanks to You, O God. We thank You for the shared memories of joy and service. We thank You for everything about _____ that made others care for him and enjoy his friendship.

[A time to mention some specific characteristics that made the friend unique and some of the areas of involvement in your club or civic organization]

And we would pray for all who are closest to him/her, for his/her family and other business associates, for the other organizations that are feeling a sense of loss. May we discover in this moment the preciousness of life and commit ourselves to make a difference in the time You have given us to live.

Pray and watch what develops!

LABOR/MANAGEMENT DISPUTE

Today we are praying about a dispute between labor and management that could disrupt jobs, and lives, and the very fabric of our nation. When we are not involved directly, answers seem easy. But we know that answers do not come easily, that tensions can result in hate and violence.

So we pray for those who are directly involved. May they be aware of Your willingness to help and then rely upon Your Spirit to direct them.

A-1

Other books by Joy Publishing:

A business guide to **Copyright Law**
What You Don't Know Can Co$t You!
by Woody Young $14.95
An easy to understand guide with all necessary forms.

Christian Writers Market Guide
by Sally E. Stuart $18.95
Info. on publishers & editors addresses & phone # plus hints

100+ Party Games
by Sally E. Stuart and Woody Young $7.95
Wholesome games for all ages & group sizes

100+ Craft & Gift Ideas
by Sally E. Stuart and Woody Young $9.95
Fun & easy ideas for parties & holidays

Secrets of Life Every Teen Needs to Know
Dr. Terry Paulson and Sean Paulson $6.95
Favorite family lectures written for teens

write His answer
by Marlene Bagnull $6.95
Devotionals that minister to writers

So You've Been Asked To Lead A Meeting
by Dr. John B. Toay and Woody Young
Due to be released - June 1991
Everything you need to know to lead a high quality meeting